TWO TRUTHS AND A MYTH

THE BATTLE OF THE Alamo

SPOT THE MYTHS

by Megan Cooley Peterson

CAPSTONE PRESS
a capstone imprint

Published by Capstone Press, an imprint of Capstone
1710 Roe Crest Drive, North Mankato, Minnesota 56003
capstonepub.com

Library of Congress Cataloging-in-Publication Data is
available on the Library of Congress website.
ISBN: 9781669087014 (hardcover)
ISBN: 9781669086963 (paperback)
ISBN: 9781669086970 (ebook PDF)

Summary: In March 1836, a group of Texan rebels were inside the Alamo. They were
fighting for independence from Mexico. When Mexican forces attacked, the Texans
were greatly outnumbered. The men defended the Alamo in a brave fight. Soon
myths were told about this famous event. Did William Barret Travis draw a line in
the sand and ask defenders to cross it? Did the Mexican troops spare any defenders'
lives? Now it's up to you to separate the truths from the myths. Will you be able to
guess them, or will you be fooled?

Editorial Credits
Editor: Carrie Sheely; Designer: Elyse White; Media Researcher: Jo Miller;
Production Specialist: Tori Abraham

Image Credits
Alamy: Everett Collection Historical, 12, INTERFOTO, 14, Science History Images,
28, The Protected Art Archive, 13, 17; AP Images: Harry Cabluck, 27; Getty Images:
mikroman6, 7, ZU_09, 8; Granger: Sarin Images, 22; Library of Congress, cover,
25, James Herring, 20, The Lyda Hill Texas Collection of Photographs in Carol
M. Highsmith's America Project, 4; Shutterstock: rylansamazingphotography, 19,
Stephen B. Goodwin, 23; Superstock: Artist - Frederick Coffay Yohn/3LH-Fine
Art, 15, ClassicStock, 21, World History Archive/Image Asset Management, 29;
Wikimedia: Texas State Library and Archives Commission, 10, 16, Texas State
Capitol, 18

Design Credits
Shutterstock, liu_miu, owatta, Quang Vinh Tran

Printed and bound in China. 6098

TABLE OF CONTENTS

Words in **bold** are in the glossary.

What Really Happened at the Alamo?

It's March 6, 1836. In the early dawn, a bugle plays outside a Spanish **mission** called the Alamo in San Antonio, Texas. Inside, about 200 Texan **rebels** race to defend the Alamo. They are fighting for independence from Mexico. They want Texas to be its own country.

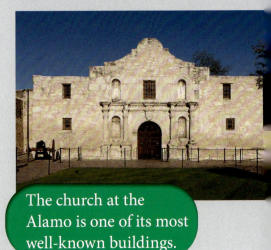

The church at the Alamo is one of its most well-known buildings.

Months before, the Texans had driven Mexican troops out of San Antonio. But Mexican forces returned. They surrounded the Alamo and its defenders for 13 days. On March 6, Mexican forces attacked. This battle was part of the Texas Revolution (1835–1836).

After the battle, myths were born. How much do you know about what happened at the Alamo? Three statements will be presented together. But only two are true. Do your best to decide what's truth and what's a myth. How well will you play the game?

HOW CAN I TELL WHAT'S TRUTH AND WHAT'S A MYTH?

START HERE. ⇨

Does the statement include words like "all" or "none"?

YES ⇨ It might be a myth. Words such as "all" or "none" often simplify complicated topics. These statements might not be true.

NO ⇨ Does the statement include specific information, such as names or dates?

YES ⇨ It might be true. Details are important when dealing with facts. The more details a statement provides, the more likely it is to be true.

NO ⇨ It might be a myth. Vague facts without detail might be made up. It's good to question statements that don't include specific details.

Before the Battle

1. SHOTS WERE FIRED AT A TEXAN PORT IN DECEMBER 1831.

Three Texan ships tried to pass through a port on the Trinity River without paying taxes. Shots were fired. A Mexican soldier was wounded. This act caused tension between Texas and the Mexican government to grow.

2. THE MEXICAN GOVERNMENT TRIED TO TAKE THE TEXANS' LAND AND COTTON PROFITS.

Texan cotton farmers were making a lot of money. The Mexican government demanded a share in cotton profits. They even took back some of the farmers' land.

San Antonio was founded in 1718 and steadily grew.

3. MEXICAN TROOPS NEEDED TO TAKE BACK SAN ANTONIO.

In December 1835, Texan fighters forced Mexican troops from the city. San Antonio had more than 2,000 citizens. It was a center of trade and business. To stop the rebellion, the Mexican army needed to regain control of the city.

THE MYTH

THE MEXICAN GOVERNMENT TRIED TO TAKE THE TEXANS' LAND AND COTTON PROFITS.

Many American **immigrants** moved to Texas to grow cotton. They **enslaved** people and forced them to work in their fields for no pay. The American immigrants treated enslaved people very poorly. Most enslaved workers were Black people. Farmers grew rich using forced labor.

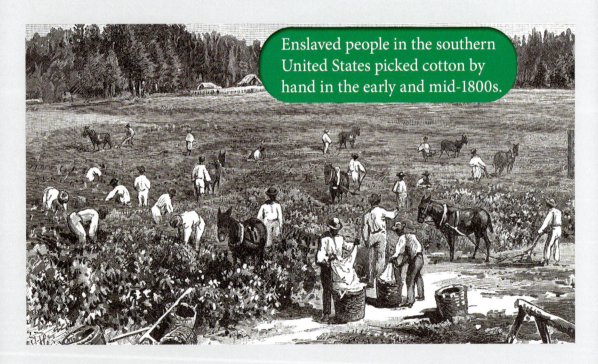

Enslaved people in the southern United States picked cotton by hand in the early and mid-1800s.

In 1827, the Mexican state of Coahuila outlawed slavery. Texas was part of Coahuila. In 1829, slavery was **abolished** in all of Mexico. Texas cotton farmers complained. Fearing rebellion, Mexican authorities allowed Texans to keep their enslaved workers.

Texans claimed the government tried to steal their "property." But they didn't mean their land or their cotton. They meant their enslaved workers. The Mexican government wanted to set enslaved people free.

FACT

A law passed in 1832 closed a loophole that allowed slavery in Texas. Using this loophole, Texans called enslaved workers **indentured servants**. They made them sign lifelong contracts.

The Defenders

TRUTH OR MYTH?

1. AMERICAN MEN CAME TO TEXAS TO FIGHT IN THE TEXAS REVOLUTION.

Many American fighters came from southern U.S. states. They were promised money and land in Texas if they won. One group from Louisiana called themselves the New Orleans Greys. The Missouri Invincibles came from St. Louis, Missouri.

2. SOME ALAMO DEFENDERS HAD MEXICAN ANCESTRY.

Many of the defenders with Mexican **descent** were born and raised in Texas. Some served under the command of Texas-born Juan Seguín.

Juan Seguín

3. WILLIAM BARRET TRAVIS DREW A "LINE IN THE SAND."

Travis was the commander at the Alamo. Before the battle, he drew a line in the sand with his sword. He asked his men to step over it if they wanted to stay and fight. All the men did except for one, who was allowed to leave.

FACT

While at the Alamo, Travis wrote a letter to ask other Texans for help fighting the Mexican army. It is kept at the Texas State Library and Archives in Austin, Texas.

THE MYTH

WILLIAM BARRET TRAVIS DREW A "LINE IN THE SAND."

Travis probably never drew a line in the sand. He knew the Alamo couldn't be defended. It was almost 0.25 mile (0.40 kilometer) around. With only about 200 men, it was impossible to defend. The Alamo itself was falling apart. Texas army general Sam Houston even gave Alamo leaders the option to destroy the Alamo.

Antonio López de Santa Anna

Antonio López de Santa Anna was president of Mexico and general of the army. According to reports by Santa Anna's officers, Travis offered to surrender to Mexican forces. But Santa Anna said the surrender had to be unconditional. This meant the men's lives may not be spared. Travis would not agree to that.

The story of Travis drawing a line in the sand has been told for many years.

The men had no choice but to stay and fight. Some defenders fled the Alamo during fighting. They were chased down and killed.

The Mexican Army

1. THE MEXICANS' GUNS WERE LESS ACCURATE THAN THE TEXANS' GUNS.

Most Mexicans carried India Pattern muskets. They could only hit targets up to about 300 feet (90 meters) away. The Texans' Kentucky long rifles were accurate to about 600 feet (180 m).

Kentucky long rifle

2. ABOUT HALF THE SOLDIERS IN THE MEXICAN ARMY WERE INEXPERIENCED.

Some of these inexperienced troops were brand-new soldiers. Professional soldiers made up the rest of the army.

General Santa Anna's orders were to kill everyone inside the Alamo. Some of the defenders' wives and children were also there. No one was spared, not even the women and children.

Both sides at the Alamo fought with guns and knives. They also used blades called bayonets that were attached to guns.

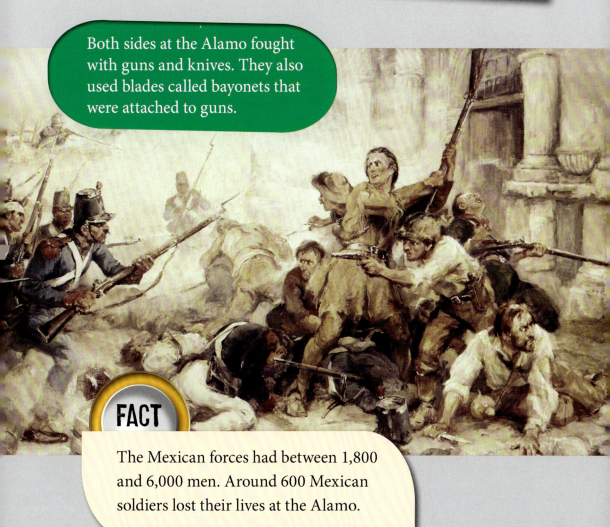

FACT

The Mexican forces had between 1,800 and 6,000 men. Around 600 Mexican soldiers lost their lives at the Alamo.

THE MYTH

MEXICAN SOLDIERS LEFT BEHIND NO SURVIVORS.

Mexican soldiers killed nearly every defender at the Alamo. But they did leave behind some survivors. Almost 20 women and children were spared, mostly of Mexican descent. Defenders Jim Bowie and William Travis had enslaved people with them at the Alamo. A man named Joe was enslaved by Travis. Bowie had one or two enslaved people too. Joe and most of the other enslaved people survived. One enslaved woman is said to have been killed during the fighting.

Susanna Dickinson was one survivor. Susanna was married to Lieutenant Almaron Dickinson. During the fighting, she hid inside the church with her baby. Other women and children also hid there.

Susanna Dickinson

Mexican army leaders spoke to survivors after the Battle of the Alamo.

Santa Anna kept Joe and Susanna in custody. He wanted them to make new lives for themselves in Mexico. Joe escaped a few days later.

Five days after the battle, Santa Anna let Susanna leave. One of his servants took her to the town of Gonzales. Sam Houston was there gathering more troops. Santa Anna sent her as a warning. Santa Anna wanted Houston to know his men would also be killed if they didn't surrender.

Famous Texan Fighters

TRUTH OR MYTH?

1. JIM BOWIE SPENT THE BATTLE IN HIS SICKBED.

Bowie had a high fever. He was also vomiting and had diarrhea. Bowie may have caught **typhoid**, likely from something he drank. Mexican troops killed Bowie in his bed.

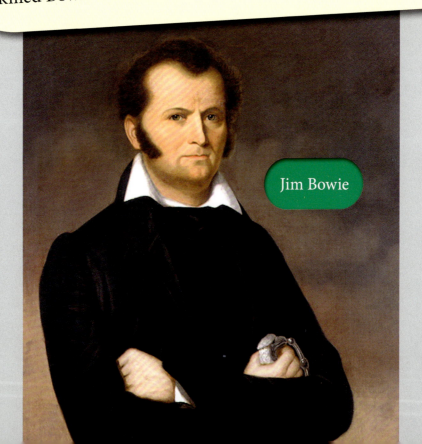

Jim Bowie

2. AMERICAN FRONTIERSMAN DAVY CROCKETT DIED FIGHTING.

Crockett ran out of bullets sometime during the battle. But he refused to quit fighting. He used the butt of his gun as a weapon.

FACT

Jim Bowie was famous even before the Battle of the Alamo. He and his brother invented a large knife called the Bowie knife.

3. WILLIAM BARRET TRAVIS DIED IN THE FIRST FEW MINUTES OF FIGHTING.

Travis was shot in the forehead while standing on the northern wall. He tumbled down a dirt ramp. He died with his sword in his hand.

THE MYTH

AMERICAN FRONTIERSMAN DAVY CROCKETT DIED FIGHTING.

During the first 10 years after the battle, many accounts said Crockett died fighting. But stories that spread in the first days after the battle tell a different story. They say Davy Crockett surrendered and was killed. Juan Almonte, a Mexican colonel, also wrote about this version of Crockett's death.

Davy Crockett

There are differing accounts of survivor Susanna Dickinson's story. At first, she said she hid inside the church during the battle. She saw none of the fighting. Later, others who heard her story said she had witnessed Crockett's death. According to the witnesses, she saw Crockett use his gun as a club when he ran out of bullets.

It's possible Davy Crockett went down fighting. But no one can say for sure what really happened. What is certain is that Crockett died at the Alamo.

Crockett's actions and how he died at the Alamo remain a mystery.

Fighting at the Battle

TRUTH OR MYTH?

1. SANTA ANNA'S TROOPS MADE 28 LADDERS TO CLIMB THE ALAMO'S WALLS.

The Mexican troops built ladders out of sticks tied together with rawhide. Most fell apart when the soldiers tried to climb them. Defenders shot down at them.

2. MANY TEXANS WENT TO THE LONG BARRACK TO HIDE.

The Long Barrack was the strongest building inside the Alamo. It was made of stone. Mexican soldiers broke down the doors. Men battled in bloody hand-to-hand combat.

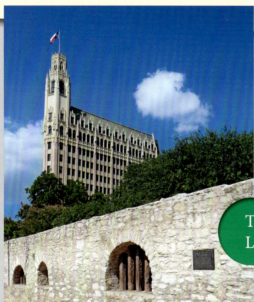

The Alamo's Long Barrack

3. THE ALAMO DEFENDERS BOUGHT SAM HOUSTON TIME TO RAISE AN ARMY.

The men defending the Alamo knew they would almost certainly lose. They kept fighting while Houston found more men for the Texas army.

THE MYTH

THE ALAMO DEFENDERS BOUGHT SAM HOUSTON TIME TO RAISE AN ARMY.

Sam Houston was in Gonzales, Texas, gathering men to help defend the Alamo after the battle. Gonzales was about 70 miles (113 km) from the Alamo. Houston didn't know the battle had taken place. Soon, two men who had witnessed the Alamo's destruction arrived in Gonzales. They broke the news that the Alamo had fallen.

Houston sent scouts to the Alamo to make sure. Along the way, they met survivors Joe and Susanna Dickinson. They confirmed the Alamo had been lost.

Houston still didn't have enough men to fight Santa Anna. Mexican troops outnumbered his nine to one.

Sam Houston

After the Battle

1. SAM HOUSTON'S TROOPS SET THE TOWN OF GONZALES, TEXAS, ON FIRE.

Everyone in Gonzales abandoned the town. They were afraid Santa Anna was on his way there. Houston ordered the town to be burned. He didn't want to leave anything behind that might help the Mexicans.

2. "REMEMBER THE ALAMO!" BECAME A RALLYING CRY FOR HOUSTON'S FIGHTERS.

Houston's men had a common purpose after the Alamo. They wanted revenge for the fallen defenders. They used this rallying cry during their next battle with Santa Anna.

3. THE ALAMO DEFENDERS DIDN'T KNOW TEXAS HAD DECLARED INDEPENDENCE FROM MEXICO AND DIDN'T THINK IT WAS LIKELY.

Texas leaders declared independence from Mexico on March 2. This news hadn't yet reached the Alamo defenders. The Alamo fighters didn't think the declaration was going to happen.

A Texas state worker holds the last signature page of the Texas Declaration of Independence.

THE MYTH

THE ALAMO DEFENDERS DIDN'T KNOW TEXAS HAD DECLARED INDEPENDENCE FROM MEXICO AND DIDN'T THINK IT WAS LIKELY.

On March 2, 1836, Texas officials adopted a declaration of independence from Mexico. The men at the Alamo probably didn't know the declaration had been officially adopted. But they knew it was likely to happen. Travis even wrote about independence in a letter he sent on March 3.

Sam Houston rode on horseback during the Battle of San Jacinto.

Houston and his men fought Mexican forces at San Jacinto on April 21, 1836. The Texans won and captured Santa Anna the next day. The Mexican president later signed a **treaty** with the Texans. It ended the war and gave Texas independence from Mexico. In 1845, Texas joined the United States as the 28th state.

Nearly 200 years ago, Texan and Mexican troops clashed at the Alamo. Since then, many myths about the battle have been told. How many myths did you pick out on your adventure?

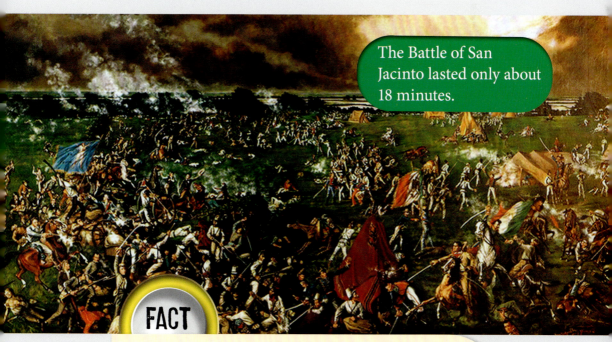

The Battle of San Jacinto lasted only about 18 minutes.

FACT

Santa Anna was napping on the afternoon of April 21, 1836, while Texans prepared to attack. His men were not ready for battle.

GLOSSARY

abolish (uh-BOL-ish)—to put an end to something officially

descent (di-SENT)—the origin or family background of a person

enslave (en-SLAYV)—to force someone to do work without pay

immigrant (IM-uh-gruhnt)—a person who leaves one country and settles in another country

indentured servant (in-DEN-churd SUR-vuhnt)—a person who works for someone else for a period of time in return for payment of travel and living costs

mission (MISH-uhn)—a church or other place where people from a religious group live and work as they try to spread their faith

rebel (REB-uhl)—someone who fights against a government or the people in charge of something

treaty (TREE-tee)—an official agreement between two or more groups or countries

typhoid (TYE-foid)—a serious infectious disease with symptoms of high fever and diarrhea that sometimes leads to death

READ MORE

Gagne, Tammy. *Texas*. Minneapolis: Core Library, an imprint of Abdo Publishing, 2023.

Levy, Janey. *The Alamo*. New York: Gareth Stevens Publishing, 2025.

Troup, Roxanne. *The Alamo*. Lake Elmo, MN: Focus Readers, 2024.

INTERNET SITES

The Alamo
thealamo.org

History.com: Battle of the Alamo
history.com/topics/latin-america/alamo

National Geographic Kids: Texas
kids.nationalgeographic.com/geography/states/article/texas

INDEX

ABOUT THE AUTHOR

Megan Cooley Peterson is a writer, editor, and bookworm. When she isn't writing or reading, you can find her watching movies or planning her next Halloween party. She lives in Minnesota with her husband and daughter.